Garth Brooks on Life, Love, and Mu

To say Garth Brook is a superstar is a major understatement. Brooks is the best selling solo artist in history with more than 130 million albums sold worldwide. Since he released his debut album in 1989, *Garth Brooks*, he has been a mainstay on country music charts.

What follows are quotes spoken by Brooks on all aspects of his life. Each quote is attributed to its original source so you can see it wasn't pulled out of thin air. Hope you enjoy reading the gems that Brooks has shared in the past 20+ years. As a bonus, after the Brooks quotes you'll find a smattering of quotes about Garth Brooks spoken by those in the music industry and those who know him best.

Table of Contents:

Life

Love

Music

Quotes About Garth

(The Love quotes involve not only the women in his life but also his daughters and parents.)

LIFE

"This town has been very cool to us, so I get to go out and I get to go to the feed store and I get to go to the grocery store.

To be honest with you, man, this isn't real life that I'm living. No matter how many trips to the grocery store you make, doing this for a living isn't real life. You've just got to grab your moments when you can and take as much from them as you can."

On living in a town near Nashville and his life. The Record, December 1994

"I was a huge rock fan in high school, and because we weren't allowed to date till we were 16, I went where my older brothers went, and they weren't into country music. But I couldn't sing the stuff I liked, no way. Even now, I believe no mortal human being can get away with doing that for very long. When I heard George (Strait), it hit me all of a sudden. I loved that sound, and the way country (writers and fans) never lost the value of the lyric, the way rock did after the 1970s."

On his musical experiences and thoughts in high school and early adulthood. Toronto Star, January 1992

"I don't know, man. We just follow our heart."

On where he sees his music headed. The Province, January 1992

"I'm actually in the middle of taking six months off, and I've shaved every day for the past 2 1/2 years. I'm just giving my face a break."

On his bearded look in 1992. Calgary Herald, January 1992

"I love to eat. You know, my resume, before I got my music job, when it says, you know, name your favorite hobbies. Eating and napping always was mine and never could find a job doing that. Now I finally have."

On liking to eat. Interview with Larry King, December 10, 2010

"I see these things in here and all I can think of is what the hell am I doing here? It's amazing. Hopefully, time will answer that question. It always does."

On mementoes from his singing career exhibited at the Smithsonian Institution. Prince George Citizen, December 2007

"I was tired after two swings. I was swinging for everything I had."

On batting practice during his stint with the New York Mets. Chatham Daily News, February 2000

"I never really knew Hank Williams until I went to college. And I'll be damned if I didn't room with this kid from Oklahoma City who was a Hank Williams nut. Sometimes I had to wake him up and tell him that he wasn't in the '50s, but the '80s. He had a ton of Williams' stuff. And shoot, even if Hank was born 100 years from now, he'd still be ahead of his time. He had a timelessness to his music that I think every artist would kill for."

On getting turned on to Hank Williams when he was in college at Oklahoma State University. The Province, August 1991

"My Dad told me to get a real job and now when you see that it is actually paying the bills and paying for college, you can't tell your kids you can't make a living at it if they try hard enough."

On having a career that pays the bills. The Canadian Press, July 2012

"Between school and sports and all the things that come with children, writing works good for me to be able to do when I have my time."

On why screenwriting appeals to him. Calgary Herald, January 2002

"The only thing better than playing music is being a dad. That's the only thing better. What I am thankful for is that my mom always said it was a gift, and as long as it's going to last, it's going to last, but the day it's over, all the money in the world can't buy you another day."

On being a father. Interview with Oprah Winfrey, November 2010

"The hardest thing ever for anybody that's got children is to walk away from them. You've got that bus out there, and you hear them screaming. They've got something planned, and you've got something planned."

On one of the hardest things he has ever had to do. Minneapolis Star Tribune, October 1998

"A big part of the romanticism of starting out is, you didn't have nothing to lose, and you were going for everything. Now every time you step out, it's like you've got everything in the world to lose."

On his success. The Vancouver Sun, October 1993

"I'll name some names - I liked Tom Rush and Townes Van Zandt, Judy Collins, Joan Baez - all that stuff I got from my older brothers and sisters who grew up in the '60s."

On the strong folk influence in his music and his exposure to folk music as a youngster. The Province, August 1991

"You could feel the eyes on you but it's never been a bother, if that's the right word."

On going out in public as a celebrity. Star-Phoenix, August 1996

"January 16th is my wife's birthday, so I usually never get her anything for Christmas because of all the bargains you can get from Christmas to Jan. 16th. I thought I'd get her a bunch of those greatest-hits CDs."

On not doing his Christmas shopping until after the holidays. The Spectator, December 1994

"I firmly feel this page of my life is ending and the next page begins. And you know how competitive I am, I'll make what I do ten times bigger than anything I've done."

On turning his attention from performing concerts to a future that includes screen writing and movies like the made-for-TV holiday film with Whoopi Goldberg. New Brunswick Telegraph Journal, November 2001

"My youngest has got it. She's got the bug but she's got the goods, too. She starts playing and singing, I have to get up and leave because I spent my whole life crying. It seems the older I get, I cry at commercials."

On his daughter Allie Colleen's interest in possibly following her father into the music business. The Canadian Press, July 2012

"Garth bashers."

On what Garth calls people who slam him. The Vancouver Sun, October 1993

"Billy Joel was a huge influence. Also James Taylor, Elton John, Boston, Kansas, George Jones, Janis Joplin - all those people I grew up listening to because of my older brothers and sister - ELO, Styx, Queen. The late '70s rock shows influenced my live shows the most, the visual stuff. Queen was unreal. I loved Kiss. Styx was cool. I had every Kiss album there was and went to the shows. What I saw was, hey, these guys aren't giving me my record or album, they're giving 'em what I don't see on albums."

On his musical tastes when growing up. Edmonton Journal, January 1992

"He died the day my mother died. He just happens to still be walking around here, and it's killing him. He'll be the first one to tell you he wishes he was gone. It's a hard one - - I'm hoping it will bring a revelation to him that he has grandchildren and children who love him and depend on him and would love to see him come back among the living."

On how his father coped after his mother's death. Calgary Herald, January 2002

"I tell them: I'm sorry, this is so new to me that I'm keeping everything."

On what he tells his fans when they ask for souvenirs during his baseball games - they want his bat, his shoes, his gloves, among other equipment. Star - Phoenix, March 1999

"To tell the truth, I feel lucky to be where I'm at in country music. It's taken everything to be competitive. I think I'll just stay here."

On his acting debut in 1991 in an episode of the NBC sitcom Empty Nest. The Gazette, October 1991

"It was awesome. It was neat to look out over the water and see the Washington Monument. Look over your right and see the future president of the United States. But the great thing about that day was we all believed in that one word, change. You talk about unity. I would wish upon the entire world the feeling that I felt all that day, unity. When you walked through there -- and, you know, one of the greatest moments of that -- and forgive me if I step on somebody's toes because I don't think this was a mistake. They said they got their timing off and I don't know if I was HBO or whatever. They did not air the prayer that opened it."

On what it was like playing at President Obama's inauguration. Interview with Larry King, December 10, 2010

"It was in 1980 and I was in my dad's car. I even remember the spot on the road when I turned on the radio and they talked about a new kid that just came out. They said, 'Here's his first single from MCA.' The song was Unwound, and it was George Strait. That pretty much right there changed my life. It's weird, man. I remember that like yesterday."

On opting to focus on country music after hearing George Strait, a new-breed country star in 1980. The Province, August 1991

"Gee, I don't know, man. We're just following our hearts."

On what he answers when asked about the secret of his sudden success in the early 90s. Edmonton Journal, January 1992

"Life is all about taking chances. Those who play it safe are going to survive but they have nothing to survive for."

On taking risks. Calgary Herald, August 1996

"I'm from Oklahoma. I know a lot about grass fires. I know a lot about wind and fire. I've never, ever seen wind and fire like I saw on the television."

On his concert in 2008 with proceeds going to the Southern California 2008 Fire Intervention Relief Effort. Prince George Citizen, January 2008

"I was even more surprised than the pitcher."

On hitting a pitch thrown by left- hander Mike Myers. Niagara Falls Review, March 2004

"What's great about the producing thing is that it's merely an assembly of great people -- I don't really need to be there, I just come in every now and then just to feel important."

On his movie production company, Red Strokes Entertainment, while he is out on tour for three years. The Spectator, April 1996

"Yes, I am, for a lot of reasons. You know, my mom and dad are gone. That's the down side. My brother Jerry's gone. So as you get older, you start to lose people. But what I have found out is people that truly lived while they were here, live forever. I see my mom every time I close my eyes. I see my mom every time I walk out on stage. So, the good things are good. As long as your children are healthy and the people you love are healthy, then everything's great. As long as your relationship with God or Christ or whatever it is you believe in is healthy, then everything's good. And I got to tell you right now, knock on wood, because I'm one of those guys that say, if you say it something -- because I love baseball and they're very superstitious; I'm kind of that way. But, yes, I can't imagine things going better for me right now."

On whether he is as happy now as he's ever been. Interview with Larry King, December 10, 2010

"We're in a situation a lot of people aren't in. Thank God we can afford to live next to each other; a lot of people can't choose where they live because their work keeps them in one place or another. We realize ours is a rare opportunity we've been given, and it's important to pass that on to the kids, because they're the ones who go through hell when marriages break up."

On parenting with his ex-wife, Sandy, and current wife Trisha Yearwood. The Canadian Press, November 2007

"I went into a Western-wear store the other day. I got my baseball cap and my sunglasses on, and a lady's across the rack from me. She goes, "I'll be damned." And her friend goes, "What's wrong?" She goes, "I come here to buy my husband a Western Shirt, and all they got are these damn Garth Brooks things." So I started sinking real low."

On everyone wearing cowboy hats and loud shirts in the '90s. Playboy magazine, May 1994

"I'm here because I'm Garth Brooks. I know that."

On his non-roster invitee to the San Diego Padres training camp. National Post, February 1999

"I feel much better. And it's funny how feeling much better physically allows my emotions and my mental things to seem to run a lot quicker, too."

On losing 50 pounds in 1994. The Ottawa Citizen, May 1994

"It's something very real where I come from. I think Oklahoma City led the world in homicides per year when I was growing up; they would average one or two a day. Violence was a way of life the same way love and happiness was. Death, after all, is as much a part of living as being born."

On violence, which has always been a way of life for Garth, a native of Yukon, Oklahoma. Kitchener - Waterloo Record, October 1991

"I still believe that I, that you, that all of us, can change the world. I think one person can make all difference in the world. Unfortunately, there have been too many bad examples where we've seen where one person can run a nation with thousands of lies. We've seen that happen . . . but I also believe it can happen for the good."

On being a dreamer. Calgary Herald, August 1996

"They're very aware. They're very sharp on those kinds of things. In our house, everyone's opinion is welcome. I grew up in a house where everything wasn't when it came to politics or religion."

On whether he talks to his daughters about political matters. Interview with Stephen L. Betts for The Boot, March 2012

"My dad was a realist; my mom is where I got my dreaming side from. But whenever I'd say to him: 'Hey Dad, we're playing for 18,000 people tonight and what do you say about that?' he'd say: 'Just remember, that's 18,000 people you could disappoint.' That tends to keep things real."

On not taking his fame for granted, which he credits to his parents, especially his dad's non-diva attitude. Prince George Citizen, November 2007

"That (his alleged marketing expertise) has been a big kind of myth, and I don't know if it's from our (his publicists') side or what. But I never majored in marketing. I got an advertising degree, and I flunked (an entry-level) marketing course three years in a row. Marketing just never was my bag. I was taking 4000 and 5000-level marketing courses while I was flunking the first one. They got past the rules and into "Marketing, What Is It?' What I learned was that the most important thing you can do is sell your next product, not the one you're selling now. If all you're doing is trying to sell your current product, you're starting over every time. Anybody can go out there and have something new that has an impact and then dies. The thing you want to do is keep the impact up. For instance, if you're selling T-shirts, you hopefully give people a T-shirt of such good quality and such good printed design that they're looking for the next one to come out."

On the marketing training he received at Oklahoma State University and its role in his stardom. Kitchener - Waterloo Record, October 1993

"Man, Queen was unreal. My ears are still hurtin' and that was 17 years ago."

On a Queen concert he went to as a youth. The Province, January 1992

"I don't know, man. I'm really a son and I'm a husband and that's what I am. But I think the person that we're here talking about right now isn't the husband and son as much as it is this guy back here, you know. The performer."

On why Garth sometimes talks about Garth Brooks as if he is another person. Calgary Herald, January 1992

"I'm excited, I'm nervous, I'm scared, and it's going to be neat. Make no mistake about it, I'm out there to play baseball."

On playing baseball with the San Diego Padres. Star - Phoenix, February 1999

"Right now I think I'm probably stepping into the fighting part of my life. I love conflict, I love emotion and I love the fight. All that means is that your blood's running and that you're not just sitting there and taking it.'"

On his life in 1995. Calgary Herald, December 1995

"That also explains the weight thing because I eat for both of them."

On trying to separate Garth Brooks the performer from Garth Brooks the husband and father. The Province, January 1992

"That's because the English language originated in Oklahoma. Didn't it?"

On why he has no accent despite being from Oklahoma. Calgary Herald, January 1992

"You know I met him backstage and he's the nicest, sweetest guy, soft-spoken. But if I went on you know he'd rip me up. Give me Don Rickles."

On why he won't be on the David Letterman show.
Edmonton Journal, December 1995

"I got to hide behind raising money for kids to get to realize a life's dream of playing baseball."

On playing baseball with the San Diego Padres in exchange for a donation to Garth's charity foundation. The Province, August 1999

"Like Allen (Reynolds, his producer and close friend) said, you can't fool the people forever. If it's going to last, it's got to be from the heart. For example, I enjoy being sad. There's a guy out there, some people call him bubblegum, but I love his stuff: Dan Fogelberg. He writes stuff that gets you so down there. I like that. It's like in the movie The Best Little Whorehouse In Texas, there's a scene where Burt Reynolds looks at Dolly Parton and says: "Dammit, I'm in a bad mood and I'd like to enjoy it." I enjoy clouds as much as I do sunshine. I love being away from someone you love and it hurts like hell but then it feels so good to be back. I love rainy days, all those things that have that dark overtone that everyone usually considers to be sad and something you don't want to deal with. I enjoy that as much as the good times. We have a saying on the back of one of our T-shirts that says: A mistake is not a mistake if a lesson is learned. So, no matter how sad a song may be, it's like real life. I went through that, man, it was tough, but I'm the better for it. That's just real life and that's what our music is to me. I want to get all kinds of emotions across to people."

On emotions and music. Calgary Herald, August 1996

"I really wasn't looking forward to it. I was scared to death. I didn't think I'd be a good father and I didn't think that I really knew what love was enough to take care of a child. My theory has always been, If you don't go out to be the best there is, why dress up and go out at all? And I knew there was no way I could be the dad my dad was to me. But when that kid came, it was like the instructions came with her and they were just "Love me." And, whew, that's cool. Also, my respect for my wife went up six bazillion notches. I used to think my wife was a puss. But, my God, I could never even think about going through that. If it'd been me who had the baby, I'd still be lying there today."

On how he felt when his first daughter, Taylor, was born. Playboy magazine, May 1994

"It was when we got here. It had cows on it for as long as anybody here can remember. But we're letting the fields kind of turn themselves over."

On the ranch he bought in Oklahoma in 2000 that used to be a working ranch. The Spectator, November 2001

"Radio still has only 24 hours in a day. So something has got to give, and trust me, if it's radio that gives, we'll fall hard. We've got to preserve radio."

On so many country singers needing radio attention. Toronto Star, December 1994

"Make no mistake. I'm here because I'm Garth Brooks. If I was a guy just going out with the team, I would not be treated the way I have so far. I look at the kids in the next (minor league) locker room and I know they have a long way to go. But I know everyone in the other locker room (major league) has paid some dues."

On playing with the San Diego Padres. Edmonton Journal, March 1999

"I truly think that singing is a gift from God and as long as that gift is supposed to last, it will. When it is over there is nothing I can do to save it. I try to take care of it by getting sleep, getting sunlight and fresh air. Other than that, when I go out I am hoping it is there when we start playing."

On what he does to protect his voice. The Vancouver Sun, April 1994

"I don't think you ever stop being a parent, but when we become empty nesters, well, my youngest graduates in May of 2014. So, we become empty nesters right around then, and who knows. Our business, as you know, this business is very fickle, so there might not be a hole for us. But if there is, I would love to tour again for the first time ever without guilt from being away from either your spouse or your children. Now my children are off doing their own thing, and my spouse is with me. You know we're together on tour, so I think that would be all the fun things."

On whether he'll tour again when his daughters are done high school in 2014. Interview with Robin Leech, December 2011

"I like that one the best. All the guys on the bus like that one, too."

On being called 'a thumb with a hat'. The Province, January 1992

"That's a tough one -- just lots of pictures of my girls and my parents. Dinner -- anything but seafood -- I've just never developed a taste for it."

On what he wants for Christmas. Edmonton Journal, December 1995

"I think we all ought to be. I am worried about where my children grow up, I am worried about where my children's children are growing up. It would be neat to turn the tide and know that my children's children were going to have a better life than my children. It is why I like to take on things in my career like We Shall Be Free and the Thunder Rolls."

On worrying about what the world is going to be like when his kids grow up. The Vancouver Sun, April 1994

"I'm crazy for being here. But it's not as crazy as it looks. Sure, I've embarrassed myself a hundred times out there. But for every one, there has been a time when I can hear somebody cheer and say, 'Ya!' and that means something."

On his time with the San Diego Padres. New Brunswick Telegraph Journal, March 1999

"Whenever I go to a concert, I like to see something that makes my blood run a little faster than when I walked in there. I like to surprise people."

On what he likes at concerts. The Province, January 1992

"I was offered a chance to read for a role in Kevin Costner's The Love of the Game. The role of Gus, the catcher. Truth is I don't want to play a baseball player. I want to play baseball. Maybe there will come a time in my life when I will let that go and do some celebrity things. Right now, I get to play baseball, and it's pretty cool."

On his love of playing baseball. Edmonton Journal, March 1999

"I want more than anything to be a good dad, husband, son because my folks are getting older. If music is to be a part of my future in five or ten years, then the luckiest man in the world just got luckier. But the people will decide that. If I'm still breathing after that, then I'll have to find out what my next purpose is."

On what he wants for the future. Edmonton Journal, December 1995

"I know this artist's worst nightmare is of being forgotten. I'm going to have to come face to face with that. I've never been a fan of the back half of the bell curve."

On his certainty that at age 33 his best days were behind him; referring to himself in the third person. The Province, November 2000

"I couldn't carry a Christian's shoelaces, although I believe God exists and I believe in the Bible. I'm one of those guys who says do more what I say than what I do. But it's a cool book ... you can learn a lot from that ol' thing."

On his belief in the Bible. Edmonton Journal, December 1995

"I miss the two hours, sure. And it's funny, still, every night about 9 o'clock your body gets to be jittery, fidgety, and it's pretty cool. But what I didn't know was going to happen was the other 22 hours in my day would become something that I looked forward to when I came home. Out there, you dread the other 22 hours because you're just in a place where you don't know anybody and you stay in a hotel and wait for your chance to play for your people."

On the aspects of touring that he misses. The Spectator, November 2001

"I don't know. If God came down and said "The secret of your success is . . ." I would love to hear him say music. I think it is a marriage of the music and the people. People have always taken care of me."

On the secret of his success. The Vancouver Sun, April 1994

"I don't care about it because it's become a bad word. There are three positions that used to be held in high regard, and look at them now -- lawyers, politicians, and no offense intended, journalists. You ask my heroes, and I'd say John Wayne, JFK, and Martin Luther King. And if they were alive today two of them would be totally discredited because the press would be pulling out every shred of their personal lives. But the commonality there was that they were good men, giants, but also human beings who make mistakes. And they won't let leaders do that now."

On why he won't go into politics. Edmonton Journal, December 1995

"There's something about being sad that feels good sometimes and you just want to stay in that little dump for a while and then come out of it."

On aiming for authenticity and his ability to shift from a good-time mode to exploring the darker regions of the heart. Calgary Herald, December 1995

"Forest ranger, park ranger. I wised up in high school and wanted to be a professional athlete. Then I wised up in college and wanted to an advertising major. Finally, after getting in the way of what God was wanting me to do all the time, I finally found out what I think it is I was supposed to be doing."

On what he wanted to be when he grew up. The Vancouver Sun, April 1994

"Our shows are very physical. I'm real heavy. I'm not going to be the smallest you've ever seen me."

On running to get in shape for the promotion and concerts for his Scarecrow album. New Brunswick Telegraph Journal, November 2001

"Being competitive and being compassionate, you hope that whatever's next, the goal is to make whatever you've done so far look small. So you approach it with that hunger and that passion to pull it off."

On possibly seeing his name in film credits in the future. Calgary Herald, January 2002

"Many things have changed for me since 1985, but my guitar playing ... it still sucks."

On his guitar playing. The Hamilton Spectator, September 1992

"I'm so proud of them. A really famous TV reporter went down there and they just threw her out after a few days because she was looking for the dirt. But they knew her deal and just concentrated on the business at hand, of looking after the survivors and cleaning up. They've got it down, the priorities of caring about people are solid."

On his pride regarding how people in Oklahoma handled the Oklahoma City bombings. Edmonton Journal, December 1995

"It wasn't at all for me. It was for the good guys. All those guys would do is eat, sleep, and think javelin. They'd work on it all the time, and never considered it work. Me, just hauling that damn thing down the runway was work."

On attending Oklahoma State University on a javelin scholarship. The Record, December 1995

"I'm sure you mean money. I still got my daughter and my wife, so I'm okay. I can do what I did three years ago, work for a living, minimum wage -- whatever it took to support my family. Do what I am basically doing now, trying to find something that I enjoy. It is all about supporting my family, I feel that is my role."

On what he would do if he woke up tomorrow and all his riches were gone. The Vancouver Sun, April 1994

"It depends. The Padres have made their contribution to the foundation. I can leave at any time. Would I stick around? It depends on if I'm offered that. The game is hard. If you fail seven of 10 times, you're a success. I learned here that no matter what happens, you're going to have to let things go."

On possibly forsaking his music career for a baseball career. Edmonton Journal, March 1999

"If I can find something to pull all my intensity to and all my direction and emotion into and still be a father to my children, then I will do it until the day I die. This. This will be cool. I would love it if they had to wheel me out there. They would have to prop me up and turn me on and let her go. I admire Roy Acuff for being in it forever and not ever stepping down and nobody ever saying he should step down. He always just nailed it."

On what he plans to do when he retires. The Vancouver Sun, April 1994

"I do have to be honest, it feels a lot better to fly across Texas Stadium at 190 pounds than 240 pounds. And, during the three days we shot the special, I didn't eat much, thinking every ounce might count."

On losing weight so the special effects during his last TV special would be easier to pull off. The Spectator, November 1994

"It's because these people (Mets' coaches and players) have put so much time in me. Everybody has been so sweet. Even if the pitcher you've just struck out against is just back from shoulder surgery, the guys in the dugout will say, 'That guy had some nasty stuff. That's the worst stuff I've ever seen.' And you're just hanging your head."

On not wanting sympathy for not doing better as a baseball player. Calgary Herald, March 2000

"If you're not out here to face the best, what are you going to tell your kids when you go home? I came here to play baseball. One day I will face the Big Unit (Randy Johnson) in front of a crowd. That's what I came here to do. I might be embarrassed and walk away. But that's not what I'm going to tell my kids. I'll be talking about how I hit him for a grand slam."

On his values while playing with the San Diego Padres. New Brunswick Telegraph Journal, March 1999

"Right now, if this world was split where part of 'em went to heaven, and part of 'em went to hell, you'd probably be seeing me right on the front line of people going to hell."

On his dark side. The Ottawa Citizen, October 1991

"It was the best decision for my personal life and my career. It allowed me to get my personal life and my career in a good balance."

On his self-imposed six- month layoff in 1993. The Spectator, November 1994

"You bet, I did before I was ever an artist, because I'm representing my father's name and my mother's name and I don't want anything to get back to them. I was afraid my dad would spank my butt as a kid. And the bigger fear was breaking my mom's heart."

On whether he holds himself to a higher standard of conduct when he is out in public. Playboy magazine, May 1994

LOVE

"My children and I are together every day, and every night I tuck those children in and I'm responsible for their safety and I feel good about that."

On being a father. Cambridge Reporter, October 2000

"It's a hard call for me, man, because it's Oz to the left of me and Oz to the right of me. Either one I choose, I can't lose. Music's been a wonderful lover to me and, indeed, a dream-fullfiller. But there's nothing like holding that little 11 pounds of flesh and blood. Man, she's golden."

On the balance between music and his baby daughter, Taylor. The Hamilton Spectator, October 1992

"He can't be a boy. We've got a girls-only bus."

On their impending third child. The Record, December 1995

"I don't want this to be what people remember of me. I must have been in a very dark, dark place with the passing of my mother (in August 1999) and the dissolving of a relationship that had been the majority of my adult life. That song helped me through it to write things more reflective of who I am."

On writing the lyrics to a song, If You Ever Wonder, about a defeated man staying in a marriage for the sake of his children, that he didn't finish. New Brunswick Telegraph Journal, November 2001

"I want them to get a college education and then, whatever they want. But my mom was on Capitol Records and my sister was the best singer in the family, and now that I'm married to Miss Yearwood, I do realize that females work ten times harder to get half as much as men. It'll break my heart if she goes into music for that reason alone, but if it gives her one-billionth of the joy it's brought me, then I wish that upon her."

On his daughter(s) possibly going into the music industry. The Canadian Press, November 2007

"I'm gonna be sad. I'm gonna need a lot of energy tonight from those people."

On needing to turn to his concert audience for consolation when he had to send his two daughters back home to his then-wife, Sandy, as she was missing them. Star-Phoenix, August 1996

"I never, ever thought in my life I'd say this, but music is not the first thing in my life anymore. Those girls somehow come along and they just take your energy and all of a sudden all you want to do is you want to do things that make them smile."

On being a dad; his girls were three, five, and seven at the time. Tribune, December 1999

"I've got to decide - and it's between me and God - if I am going to be able to tour and be a dad. If one has to suffer from the other, it can't be my daughter."

On making music after becoming a father in 1992. Kitchener - Waterloo Record, September 1992

"I asked my wife to be both mother and father for eight years to our three daughters and it's time for me to accept my responsibilities as a parent."

On Sandy and parenthood. Cambridge Reporter, October 2000

"The only thing I have to go off of is my own childhood and what my parents did. And the one thing I remember most from that time was, my dad worked six or seven days a week, two jobs. I played sports all the time, and sometimes I would start and some times I wouldn't. Sometimes the games would be 200 miles (320 kilometres) away from home, and sometimes they'd be on a weekday. But no matter where it was, or when it was, I would look around and I would see those two people in the stands. The greatest gift my folks gave me was time and attention. That's what I feel I owe my child. And if it costs me my music career, you know, I think God gave me my music career. And God could be telling me it's time to let it go."

On his childhood. Kitchener - Waterloo Record, September 1992

"Every decision you make, if it concerns two of you, make it from the other side."

On advice when asked about love. The Province, November 1997

"I'm keeping no secrets from anybody. Sandy and my relationship is more honest than it's ever been. And my relationship with my three children, I'm here every second they turn around."

On the key to his happiness in the early 2000s. New Brunswick Telegraph Journal, November 2001

"It's not official yet. But Sandy thinks she is and her instincts are usually correct."

On Sandy possibly being pregnant with baby #3. The Record, December 1995

"I am known around this town as 'Taylor's dad' or 'Augusts' dad' or 'Allie's dad'."

On how things are with the people around his home, a ranch 25 minutes north of Tulsa, Oklahoma. New Brunswick Telegraph Journal, November 2001

"Our youngest - that's the one Miss Yearwood keeps saying is dangerously talented."

On his daughter, Allie's naturally gifted singing ability. The Canadian Press, November 2007

"Probably the biggest thing came with a discussion with my guitar player. He said, 'I celebrated my daughter's one-year birthday today. I called her.' And we sat down and figured out he had seen that child 49 days of her first year. That's when I said enough is enough. Family was here before all this happened and family will be the only thing left after all this happens. Let's take care of family."

On his six-month sabbatical in 1991. Calgary Herald, January 1992

"It's perfect with the kids the ages they are. Obviously, things will have to change as they get older."

On touring with his family in tow. Calgary Herald, January 1997

"Here, you sleep with your children, you get up and fix them breakfast, you know where they're at, you know they're safe and you're not running from your responsibilities."

On being there for his three daughters -- Taylor, August, and Allie. The Spectator, November 2001

"It didn't work, but Sandy's practically next door to her parents, I'm practically next door to her and the kids are happy. Sandy's happy. So the plan is for the next at least 13 years, I'll be here when my children go to school and just try to do the best I can."

On moving back to Sandy's hometown to try and salvage their marriage. The Spectator, November 2001

"It was as simple as putting my family first. Now every minute I don't spend with my family I spend with music, not the other way around."

On family taking the priority over music. The Province, December 1994

"The characters are interchangeable, but you have to pick one when you write. For some reason, doing a woman made it stronger for me. I'm not sure it's not both of us. I'm not sure it's not anybody who's been in that situation."

On writing The Storm on his Scarecrow CD and whether it's his story or his ex's. New Brunswick Telegraph Journal, November 2001

MUSIC

"There's no story here about Garth wanting to break out of country. There's no story here about Garth getting so fed up he's got to stretch out."

On his Chris Gaines stint, spoken in the third person as he sometimes does. National Post, September 1999

"I enter this break with a smile. And the last break I entered very tight-lipped, my fists clenched, and not knowing what was waiting on the other side. I didn't have my priorities straight, to be honest with you. I had family second, career first. So I got my priorities straight."

On his impending 1995 break from the music industry. The Record, December 1994

"Gaines is very much like the Braveheart of music. He believes and fights for his stuff and his fans so hard that it will eventually cost him his life. That's what I think I grew to love about this guy."

On Chris Gaines. Niagara Falls Review, September 1999

"The last thing that I really need from (the press), and I'm praying that you really hear me on this, (is that) I don't want it to be called the last record, the farewell record. Could this possibly at this point be my last record? Yes, it could. But do I want to sell a record on the fact that it's the last record, or the farewell record? No."

On his retirement and the announcement of a new CD in 2001. Expositor, November 2000

"I think you must surround yourself with those people. As much as you hate the truth sometimes."

On working with family members and old friends who keep him from getting a swelled head. The Record, December 1994

"If they choose to sit this one out, I can't complain. We've had a wonderful decade thanks to them and God, and hopefully there is something we can bring them in the future that we can dance again to."

On some Garth fans opting out of listening to his Chris Gaines music. The Standard, September 1999

"That was to raise money for somebody and tickets were 45 bucks, which I thought was crazy."

On what Brooks thought was a high cost for a ticket to attend one of the concerts played at the Staples Center in Los Angeles in 2009 to benefit firefighters and victims of the Southern California wildfires that had raged the previous fall. Calgary Herald, October 2009

"If people tune in, it's going to put us in front of ten times as many people as it took us three years to see live on tour. So it works out really well for me as a father. . . . It makes us feel very good and very confident going into the season of the Scarecrow."

On his three concert specials on CBS in 2001. Daily Mercury, November 2001

"Can you tell me what I'm looking for that I don't already have? Has anybody sold more?"

On claims by the critics that his foray into Chris Gaines is an attempt to abandon country music for pop stardom. Niagara Falls Review, September 1999

"It takes six months to make a record. And you're in with guys that believe that if you're supposed to be in (the recording studio) until four in the morning, you will be. Because music comes first, at that time."

On making a record. Expositor, November 2000

"The greatest thing about '70s rock 'n' roll was that this one format stood up on the mountain and said, 'To all who feel they have something that's cool, bring it to me and we will play it'. Now country music sits up on top of this hill, and it says, 'To all who think their music is cool, bring it to me and we will play it.' And that's cool, because 10 years ago country music wouldn't have done that. Billy Ray Cyrus would've been laughed at and the door would've been closed on him."

On country music in the early 1990s. Kitchener - Waterloo Record, September 1992

"If you've ever been into a fight, or you've ever been into an athletic thing, once you're in it, you better start giving it everything you've got to survive. I surrounded myself with people that knew what hip and cool was since I don't."

On his Chris Gaines phase. Niagara Falls Review, September 1999

"I do hear a lot of talk about the people managing him, that they have more of a rock attitude. I don't know. Everything should be Clint's choice, but I'm not sure it is. But he's a super-nice guy."

On Clint Black. Kitchener - Waterloo Record, October 1991

"The road of country music winds and twists and veers off and does things. There's a fine line between reinventing yourself again, and then selling out to try and get airplay. That's a tough line that you walk."

On the country music industry. Daily Mercury, November 2001

"It's a girl driver, all girls."

On the tour bus being a Girl's Bus during his 1995 tour. The Spectator, November 1995

"Yeah, he's somebody else."

On his larger-than-life image, captured by TV cameras swinging through a ring of fire and flying in a harness over a sea of 68,000 fans, during a filming for his concert specials in 1994. The Ottawa Citizen, January 1994

"We're trying to push home that this is not an album about Christmas. It's an album about the feelings that should be shared not only at Christmas but beyond the season. It talks about the good things we share one day a year when we should be sharing them 365 days a year."

On his album Beyond the Season. The Hamilton Spectator, October 1992

"If I'm burning a bridge with the format of country radio, I don't know it. And if I am, then I'll pay for that on the next thing, I guess, that I bring to them."

About his Chris Gaines phase. Niagara Falls Review, September 1999

"I might be totally wrong but I feel more welcome by the industry on this record than I can ever remember."

On his album Sevens. The Vancouver Sun, December 1997

"I just thank God country music is the one form left that doesn't have so many pigeonholes in it that you've got to follow or you don't get to qualify."

On country music.   Kitchener - Waterloo Record, September 1992

"With the emergence of MTV and CMT (Country Music Television), I think the attention span of the public has been shortened dramatically. I took six months off this year and it felt like starting over. So I'm not particularly fired up about taking eight months off because I know it's going to be even harder to start over."

On the impact of MTV and CMT on country music. The Hamilton Spectator, October 1992

"I can understand how people can go, 'Now wait a minute, if he's retired, how's he doing all this stuff?'   An easy way to clear it up is to point out that I'm doing exactly what I said I'd do. But that doesn't sell any papers. You know?"

On his retirement in early 2000s. Daily Mercury, November 2001

"Well, I've got personal pressure I put on myself. But as far as outside pressure, it got relieved in a gift, and the gift was a gentleman by the name of Billy Ray Cyrus. He comes along, blows out three million units in two singles, and all of a sudden it's, 'Garth who?'"

On his success following Cyrus's success; said with laughter in his voice. Kitchener - Waterloo Record, September 1992

"You go wherever it takes you. When you rely on the people, then events kind of create themselves."

On his highly successful concert in August 1997 in New York's Central Park. The Vancouver Sun, December 1997

"It's like you've got four guys on the porch in Kentucky somewhere, but the four guys are John Lennon, Paul McCartney, George Harrison, and Ringo Starr with a fiddle and harmonica."

On his song Wrapped Up in You, a catchy acoustic pop number. Daily Mercury, November 2001

"I'm a guy that always needs self-purpose. So I will find things to be involved with. Just not touring."

On his upcoming break from touring in the late 1990s. National Post, November 1998

"Till then (going to Nashville in 1985), the furthest I'd ever been was halfway to Dallas. I got scared. I'd never really been out that much. When I got to Nashville a couple of years later, I stayed 23 hours and ran back home, scared to death. I went back in 1987 with my wife, which made all the difference in the world. The world and Yukon (Garth's home town) are far, far apart. But the more I'm away, the more I realize the whole world is Yukon, Oklahoma, just on a bigger scale. It's all people striving for a dream and trying to create happiness."

On his foray to Nashville and the realizations it brought. Toronto Star, January 1992

"Smith basically said to me, 'Don't retire, man. Just take some time off and see what it's like to do that. Don't do albums, don't do nothin'. What I basically want you to do is get so bored that you want to go back on the road. Just see what it's like to retire.' So that's what we're going to try to do. I'm going to fight like hell to give this time to my wife and my little child, because when I do that, I'm really giving it to me."

On the advice given to him by Capitol Records president Joe Smith. The Hamilton Spectator, October 1992

"That will be very different for me. It will be totally night and day because it's an acting thing. It's a pop thing."

On his upcoming Chris Gaines project. National Post, November 1998

"Some of the songs are actually four cities mixed together."

On his Double Live CD. The Spectator, September 1998

"I think for their sake and Country Music Television's sake, too, I would like to see another network come out so they can push each other and compete. Whenever you have one network that totally dominates something, I'm not sure that the most is being done for the music. The Nashville Network has been wonderful to me but for the sake of the music, I'd like to see another company come out so they can compete."

On the monopoly-type nature of The Nashville Network and its affiliated video channel, Country Music Television. Edmonton Journal, January 1992

"I haven't turned into this wonderful wizard that knows everything about selling records and stuff. I'm still the kid, the guy, the bum, the kind of guy who just likes to eat and play music. I'm still a guy that just really goes to bed and goes, 'Why me?'"

On his success with music. The Hamilton Spectator, October 1992

"It's like a Cheerio. You keep pushing it down, it keeps popping up. It's sweet. I like that."

On his album Ropin' the Wind returning for the second time to the No.1 spot on the Billboard charts. Toronto Star, January 1992

"It's something that kills me. I really believe you CAN please everybody all the time if you try hard enough."

On the occasional bad review he gets. Kitchener - Waterloo Record, October 1991

"After all the excesses of the '80s, people are ready to be touched. They're ready to have something thoughtful put in front of them. They want to be able to communicate with their hearts and their minds, not just their bodies or their wallets."

On his belief that country music will continue to surge in popularity. Edmonton Journal, January 1992

"As for touring, if I can't eat it, sleep it, breathe it, then it ain't me."

On pondering touring in 2009. The Guelph Mercury, October 2009

"It's things like this that make me praise technology. The gift that AEG (Network LIVE) and participating theatres have given me is to be able to go on a virtual tour without leaving home. How does it get any better than that?"

On the concert that was simulcast live to 24 Empire Theatres locations on November 14, 2007. Now, November 2007

"If it means more to me this year, it's only because it's one more year down the road. That's only supposed to happen to cool guys like George Strait."

On being declared the best country music entertainer for the fourth time, in 1998. Daily Gleaner, September 1998

"Music is a very, very powerful thing. It's passion and emotion. I'd bet on music before I'd bet on the economy of any nation to pull us through the worst of times."

On music. Toronto Star, January 1992

"Country music is about real life. I think country music was covering real life when Jimmy Rogers was singing songs about trains ... but real life at this time is not the train songs and the prison songs. The Chase talks about stuff like date rape, talks about TV evangelism, talks about starving children, talks about prejudice against color or sexual preference. It talks about that and that's real life for me today."

On country music and his album The Chase. The Hamilton Spectator, October 1992

"We used to have the underdog edge, the surprise element, the OHMIGOD-I-didn-t-KNOW-he-was-gonna-do-THIS kind of thing. But the more you use the shock treatment, the surprise thing, the harder it is to surprise."

On what he's lost since becoming America's biggest-selling solo vocalist. Kitchener - Waterloo Record, October 1991

"We're going to take the retirement roof off over our head, and I already feel taller."

On coming out of retirement in 2009. The Guelph Mercury, October 2009

"I said, 'Guys, here's the opportunity that's come up; here's where we're at.' And when I explained it to them, all they did was look at each other. Then Taylor (Brooks' eldest child) said, 'Can we go?' I said 'Yep,' and they were in. That was it."

On discussing the possibility of accepting the offer to play at the Wynn in Las Vegas with his wife Trisha Yearwood and his three girls. Calgary Herald, October 2009

"I was saying I'd retire when I couldn't. I really couldn't. It would break my heart to retire. When I talked about retiring, it was because of family duty - debt I owed to my children and to my wife. Instead of me asking God to let me live without it, I just say thank you to God for what I've got to see."

On his declaration of retirement in 1992. Kitchener - Waterloo Record, April 1993

"It's still about entertaining people. It's still about them walking out and saying, 'Man, if he comes back here, I'll be back here.' I've pretty much stayed with that. Having fun -- that's what it's all about."

On performing. The Hamilton Spectator, October 1992

"Other than waking up to my little girls, there's no place I'm happier. There have been times I have been sick, puking my guts out on the way to the stage, but once I get on stage I'm healthy and happy."

On the emotional rush he feels going on stage.   The Record, December 1995

"I'll never make it through the song. I've been practicing night and day. The national anthem is one of the hardest songs to sing. I have to be exactly on the right beat or I'm screwed."

On singing The Star-Spangled Banner at the Super Bowl in 1993. Calgary Herald, January 1993

"Today, I am starting a new life. I am here to announce my retirement -- a thing I feel good about."

On his retirement in 2000. Prince George Citizen, October 2000

"We've had fun, we've had a lot of fun. And it's just crazy. You can't get them to quit clapping in between songs. You don't want them to stop clapping either ... they just treat me so good."

On his 2007 performances at the Sprint Center in Kansas City. The Canadian Press, November 2007

"The one thing that can keep you out there today is the material. As long as the material is there, hopefully the artist will be there. If the artist is just an asshole, material isn't going to make any difference; but if you treat people the way they want to be treated, it's the material that will make the difference."

On the current tendency of country superstardom to be a revolving door. Kitchener - Waterloo Record, October 1991

"The Lamb is still Paramount's baby, and if Paramount says we're going forward with this . . . and if they're crazy enough to let me do the soundtrack, I'll go back in and do it, even though it was the hardest thing I've ever done."

On The Lamb and his Chris Gaines project. Tribune, January 2001

"I was lucky enough to get to play Cheyenne on their 100th. When the invitation to play Calgary's 100th came in, I didn't think twice. It is an honour to play the Stampede anytime. It is a once in a lifetime chance to get to play its 100th."

On performing a concert during the Calgary Stampede's 100th anniversary in July 2012. Calgary Herald, April 2012

"Sure I'm scared to death -- I'm rusty and I've seen these young guys. But I'm a competitor and when it's game day you start competing. Keith Urban is a beautiful guy, and he's just one of about 50 guys out there I'll have to face this fall so if you don't bring your A game you're going to get run over. And I'm Mr. Yearwood now so I want to make her proud."

On returning to music after his self-imposed retirement. The Times, August 2007

"Whew! People have not forgotten, man, and to be given six months off and come back and not be forgotten is the neatest gift people have ever given me. To totally shut down TV and everything for six months and come back like you never left ... what a sweet, sweet gift."

On his return to the music industry after a six month hiatus in 1993. Kitchener - Waterloo Record, October 1993

"We were in Nebraska last year when the awards show occurred, and we had booked this Buffalo date a year-and-a-half ago. I told the CMA the only way we were going to avoid the show is if Buffalo did something extreme like sell 100,000 tickets. This kind of stuff just happens and we're thankful it does."

On not being able to attend the 1998 Country Music Awards in Nashville because he had a previous concert engagement. The Spectator, September 1998

"I feel egotistical saying this but it's not just the choruses, it's every word of every verse and it's very flattering. The acoustics are amazing in this arena, so you can hear them as clear as a bell. The reason my voice is gone is that I'm trying to hear myself over them, they're singing so loud. I love it."

On the fans singing along to every song at the Sprint Center in Kansas City in 2007. The Canadian Press, November 2007

"It's funny how a chubby kid can just be having fun and they call it entertaining."

On being voted entertainer of the year in 1991. Kitchener - Waterloo Record, October 1991

"There will be ships coming in and ships getting ready to leave, so this will be a good time to get to play for both. That makes me feel all right."

On his upcoming performance live in Norfolk, Virginia, for servicemen and women of the aircraft carrier USS Enterprise as they return from the Middle East. The Spectator, November 2001

"Johnny inducted me into the Opry 11 years ago and that's still the highest honour I've received in this business. I love him, I'm a fan, and if this show can help him get better, I'm all for it."

On Johnny Russell and the tribute performance he and other country music stars did to raise funds for Russell's medical expenses. Tribune, March 2001

"My babies come first. I think I'll probably announce my retirement at the end of the year."

On an upcoming retirement phase. Observer, December 1999

"Guys, it's a character. It's the same as Tom Hanks. He can play a lost, wonderful guy in Sleepless in Seattle, then he's a character dying of HIV in Philadelphia. I guess the thing I don't get here is people didn't sit down and write him and tell him, 'You're gay!' Chris Gaines is simply a character."

On Chris Gaines. The Spectator, September 1999

"To go from horizon to entertainer in a year . . . (means) you can go from entertainer to nobody the next year."

On his thinking that fame can be fleeting. Kitchener - Waterloo Record, April 1993

"So I was trying to find a phrase that meant thinking with your heart, and my little girls pointed it out. 'Come on, Dad, the scarecrow (from The Wizard of Oz) thought with his heart.' And that made sense, so it became the working title. What I liked about it was in no way could you find any finality in it. There was no farewellness to it."

On coming up with the name for his Scarecrow album. The Spectator, November 2001

"They've all got traditions on how to act. They have chants -- this olay, olay, olay -- that's usually used during Australian-rules football. It's more rehearsed and it's really intense. They get into it."

On his Australian fans, as he observed them during his tour. The Record, September 1994

"For those people that think country music is about, oh my, you know, I lost my wife and my dog got run over at the truck stop today, those people that think that's country music probably haven't heard country music in the last five or six years. I mean, I understand that. But people do change, and formats do change. And country music is a lot more about everyday life now than centrally focused on love, good or bad."

On country music. The Gazette, January 1992

"Yes, I don't know about staying on top, but just being competitive, staying in there. You want to better yourself. You want to be a better person. You know, ten years down the line, you can have all these things up on your wall, these plaques, all these awards, but if you're not a better musician and a better singer, songwriter, and a better person after that ten years, are you really a success? And I think that's the main thing. And after that ten years, if you don't have all those plaques and things, but you're a better person, you're not a failure. That's the important thing."

On whether it's harder to get on top or stay on top. Interview with Larry King, December 10, 2010

"I'm just hearing the old Hag (Merle Haggard) stuff again, the old George Jones, the Lefty (Frizzell) stuff, the Jerry Jeff Walker. And yeah, that's probably gonna influence me."

On songwriting in 1994 and 1995. The Gazette, August 1995

"We want to visually make it apparent that The Hits is over, so we're burying the . . . master of The Hits in L.A. in front of the towers, where it all started in 1988."

On the ceremony held in June 1995 in front of the Capitol Records office in Los Angeles with the album's master recording. The Record, June 1995

"Nine years ago you never dreamed it could get this big, but for some reason it keeps evolving, which I'm thankful for. It might be over with tomorrow but for tonight I want to dance."

On how was feeling before playing at six sold-out shows in Philadelphia in 1998. Kingston Whig - Standard, September 1998

"I do the best I can and the people decide. If they don't want it, it's termed a failure, and that's okay by me."

On the Chris Gaines project. Toronto Star, September 1999

"I've never considered myself a hip guy. That's why I stayed out of the studio on all the sessions, let (the musicians) do their thing, then I'd just go in and sing. I'd have somebody else sing the vocal rough so I could see if that's the style we all agreed on or if they wanted to take that style or make it raspier or something."

On recording the Chris Gaines music. The Province, August 1999

"It's these people out there causing havoc in the lines and showing up the night of the show, raping the fans."

On ticket scalpers. Kitchener - Waterloo Record, November 1993

"I think it might be a fear thing that people don't like their Garth doing this, and that's cool. But they need to realize there's a lot of instances like this that have happened before. Hank Williams was also Luke the Drifter. The Statler Brothers did the Road Hog (a fictional character named Lester (Roadhog) Moran). I stopped defending it so much after I played the stuff live out in California (for the television special). When the taping was through, I strapped on a guitar and played The Dance as a way to say thank you. The reaction I got to Chris was the same reaction I got to Garth. It hit me that whether it's Low Places or Chris, it's all Garth music."

On doing his Chris Gaines thing. The Spectator, September 1999

"We made a deal, Alan Reynolds (his album producer) and myself, to do what we called heart music. The one thing everybody in this world has in common, the only thing they have in common, is that they have a heart. They might not speak the same language. They might not listen to the same music. But they've all got hearts. So that's the kind of music we tried to play."

On the source of his music. Calgary Herald, January 1992

"As the years go on and the song list piles up, you can't do another Shameless, you can't do another Friends in Low Places, 'cause you've already done that."

On a couple of his past huge hits. The Gazette, August 1995

"Here, somebody hired me to do what I would eventually have done anyway (for my own enjoyment). It's not country and it's not a representation of Garth Brooks. But now somebody has given me the keys to do this and put it out as their project. But I play this CD at home and I usually don't do that with my stuff. Usually when it's through, I'm ready to take a break. But this thing, I just play it all the time."

On his Chris Gaines project. The Province, August 1999

"I wanted him to be thin, gorgeous, and (have) long hair. He's a musical genius such as Prince is a musical genius in real life. He gets depressed a lot . He's very loyal to his fans and he'll die for his music."

On how he sees Chris Gaines. Toronto Star, September 1999

"I spend all my time right now trying to combat music retail and copyright. Because if I'm going to enter back into this race when the girls go off to college, right now there's no reason to make new music other than the fact that you want to make new music. The way the system is set up, it's impossible. I unfortunately have been working on that. I can't wait to get that behind me. Hopefully, between digital spaces like iTunes and YouTube, we'll get our end figured out, because they're not going to do it for us. No offense to anybody. We just need to get our collective stuff together and if we do that, I can enjoy a possible shot at a second half of a run. But until that happens, I've got nothing planned."

On whether he is working on any new music. Interview with Stephen L. Betts for The Boot, March 2012

"I think we're in a no-lose situation. If we get pounded, it's by the Beatles and everyone's expecting us to get pounded anyway. And if for some reason we hold our own, it's going to make country music, make Garth Brooks, look stronger. So we'll see."

On Fresh Horses arriving in record stores at the same time as a double CD of Beatles music, including the first new Fab Four song in 25 years. The Spectator, November 1995

"I think the purpose of this special is pretty much to show what the last two years has done. The music is from the last two years. And I'm hopin' for the people that saw the first special, what they say here is, hey, it doesn't seem the guy has changed that much."

On his TV special, This is Garth Brooks Too, that ran on NBC in 1994. The Ottawa Citizen, May 1994

"I'm having the time of my life. I mean, there's a feelin' you get when there's just two people in the room. Well, I gotta be honest with you, there's been times when there's 17,000 people in the room -- it's a lot better feelin' than that."

On the rigours of superstardom. The Province, January 1992

"I've always been one of these guys who tries to prepare for the worst and one of the worst things that could happen would be that I'm not doing this tomorrow. Being prepared for something like that keeps you pretty much tied to the ground. Besides, I don't want to get into a lifestyle that costs a lot of money. I don't want to think of myself as somebody that I'm not. This is not real life. These celebrity things come and go. It's been an unbelievable step up but the worst kind of step is the big step down. I just don't want it to be that big of a change when it's over."

On himself in the music industry. Calgary Herald, August 1996

"Man, my writing is just not - it's all in there, I just can't find it. By the time they (his and wife Sandy's two small children) go to bed, I'm worn out so I don't stay up till 4 a.m. writing like I used to. So you just dig a little deeper and the albums take a bit longer."

On having trouble writing for a new album in 1995. The Gazette, August 1995

"Now with 50-something channels on TV, 80,000 something channels on the radio, the Web, the Internet, people are having their attention pulled away."

On how he finds it is getting harder to let people know you have something out. The Hamilton Spectator, May 1996

"It was tough to get back in the game. It's still hard to get back in the game. I was out two years and now I've been back three weeks, and I find it's not like riding a bike. I thought this gig would get easier and instead it's just getting harder and harder. The next album is going to be 10 times harder to make than this one. So now begins really the hardest part yet of the journey: trying somehow to keep this thing feeling like it's new and the answer lies in the people."

On going back on tour after a break. The Record, December 1995

"I only have one intention, and that is to make people at the CMAs feel like Buffalo is the centre of the universe and say, 'Wow, they look like they're having fun tonight. I wish I was there.'"

On performing In Another's Eyes via satellite for the Country Music Awards in Nashville in 1998 from Buffalo, New York. The Spectator, September 1998

"Anything after that, if it's Chris Gaines, it's because I want to. If the demand's inside me, whether the demand's out there or not, I can make another one that I can sit at my house and play."

On what he will do once he is done the Chris Gaines CD and The Lamb movie as then he'll have fulfilled his commitment to Paramount. The Province, August 1999

"Please don't take this as egotistical but the country music audience I believe has taken Garth to a status that (any) pop (artist) would enjoy themselves. Why would I want to go to pop status when the status that they (fans) brought me to is easily what I consider pop status anyway?"

On how he responded to a critic's claims that Garth used the Chris Gaines project to test his viability as a pop artist. Toronto Star, September 1999

"Well, the problem I had the first night with flying was I didn't wear the harness throughout the whole show. So, I was running back to put it on and it took longer than I thought. So, in coming back and getting hooked up and flying, I had realized that I had forgotten to zip my pants. Nobody saw anything. But it sure was a lot cooler that night."

On the sequence during a concert in which Brooks flies through the Texas Stadium in Dallas suspended in mid-air. The Ottawa Citizen, May 1994

"Yeah, I would if 5,000 people hadn't already done it. If we do something like that, it'll be something that's been thought out, maybe a little different. I'd love to do an unplugged special in that way."

On whether he would consider doing an acoustic concert. Calgary Herald, May 1994

"People are looking for songs to learn from. Why wouldn't you rather do that than have dust gather in your veins and brain? Why not listen to something that, like, yeah man, this makes me think and it upsets me -- that's good."

On his desire to restore the meaningful lyric to contemporary music. The Province, January 1992

"If more Chris Gaines stuff is called for, it's not a guarantee it's going to be made. It's got to be made because all the players get back together because our soul is telling us we've got to play more of this music."

On whether there will be another Chris Gaines album. Toronto Star, September 1999

"We announced our retirement last November. With that statement, we said we had one album left to make (for Capitol Records) and this is it; we're turning it in. It's been a labour of love but a tear. And now we'll do our best to promote it and then the next page of our life begins."

On his Scarecrow album. The Spectator, November 2001

"Anyway, I don't even see The Fever as taking a chance. If there's anything I could tell radio, tell retail, tell anybody, is that it's just Garth Brooks. As much as The Dance is me, The Fever is me."

On country music radio being reluctant to play The Fever because of its link to Aerosmith. Calgary Herald, August 1996

"This is where everybody ties me to a tree and burns me."

On his refusal to share his career strategy. The Province,
January 1992

"When I started, I thought it had to be a be-all, end-all album.
(Producer) Allen Reynolds worked very hard to talk me out of
that. He told me to just make it a reflection of where you're at
right now, like all your other albums have been. When that
happened, the weight lifted and it sure got a lot more natural
to do and things began to clear."

On his Scarecrow album. The Spectator, November 2001

"He told me years ago that people can hear it on the radio
when someone is just reading a lyric off a sheet. So, if you're
going to sing, sing about something that means something to
you because people can tell over the radio how deep it's
coming from. Like Allen said, you can't fool the people
forever. If it's going to last, it's got to be from the heart."

On advice about making music from his good friend Allen
Reynolds. Calgary Herald, December 1995

"There was some countries, man, like Sweden, where we sold
more tickets to the concert than we'd sold records in the whole
country. It's like, reality starts to come in."

On touring in countries where he is virtually unknown.
Toronto Star, December 1994

"I heard a shocking thing the other day, that some radio programmers don't think George should be on radio, that his time has passed. And I lose my hair when I hear that because that's the guy that put me on the radio, that I fashioned myself after and was my hero. And if he's not on the radio, why am I?"

On George Jones. The Spectator, November 2001

"If I were to tell you that, I'd probably lose my job with the stockholders."

On how much he gets paid for his gig at Wynn's Encore Theatre in Las Vegas. Calgary Herald, October 2009

"If I feel that the crew is going to sleep on me during a show, I'll immediately jump from the [pre-established] set list and introduce another song. Our whole light rigging is pre-programmed — one song after another — on computers. Now the crew has to rip the program out, put a new one in, and do it all before the new song starts. So if I feel people are getting lazy or complacent we'll just take off in another direction. Some of our greatest shows have happened this way, because all of a sudden half-way though the show you can see these guys scrambling. You can see the communication going on — the headsets are on, everybody's talking and yelling, and their blood's flowing!"

On what he does if he feels his crew is sleepwalking through a show. Interview with Kevin Freiberg at the San Diego Padres spring training camp, 1999

"It's an awareness thing for the album. I've never been one to want to cram myself down anyone's throat but I owe it to the songwriters, the musicians, to the company. So it's a case of getting the message out -- it's still people's choice whether or not they're interested."

On touring for his Fresh Horses CD. Edmonton Journal, December 1995

"I would put it in an all-black cover with no pictures and explain that it's a pre-promotion for a movie and this is the character in the movie."

On the one thing he would change about his Chris Gaines compact disc. New Brunswick Telegraph Journal, November 2001

"In my opinion, there is room for one Merle Haggard tune a day on country radio to let all of us punks remember why we're here and also what we're striving for: to sound as authentic as that. Even rock 'n' roll stations play old Rolling Stones every now and then just so all of us can remember what brought us to the dance."

On his hopes that country radio opens up a bit more, not just for him but other artists who are often ignored today. Calgary Herald, December 1995

"Scared to death, and it's odd that you mention this because my wife says, this was like a month ago, "Why do you get so nervous before you go out?" I said because I don't know why these people show up, so when you don't know why something happens, you're scared to death that this time when you go up onstage, it's not going to happen. Does that make any sense? So I kind of get to take the ride along with the people because I don't even know what's coming up next.

It's stupid and silly to say that, but at the same time, it's really fun and dangerous."

On his nerves kicking up before going on stage.   Interview with Robin Leech, December 2011

"I don't get that. My thing is, I'm wondering if they mean in the '90s. That's the only thing I can think of. Because when I first heard about that, I was on live TV. And I said, 'Excuse me? Are you kidding me?' Because Michael Jackson sold more of one album (1982's Thriller) than we've sold of all five of ours . . . but it's definitely something to shoot for."

On how he's the only male solo artist in music history to have two albums each sell more than 10 million copies - 1990's No Fences (11 million in the U.S., 600,000 in Canada) and 1991's Ropin' The Wind (10 million U.S., 400,000 Canada). Toronto Star, December 1994

"The idea is to think of new ways to entertain people. Yeah, it's a war, but if you keep the music and the work first in your mind, I really believe it'll all work out."

On the next phase of his music. The Province, December 1994

"I know, I know. Strange stuff. But you have to hear the music to understand."

On putting out the Chris Gaines pop album. Vancouver Sun, July 1999

"No offence whatsoever to Pink Floyd, but it's almost like you lose the band in that. It's really cool stuff, but I just need to find a way to get that kind of technology and that show in an arena show, where the band is still prevalent, everybody still has a place, but you still get the really cool, big power tech stuff like that. I think that's the goal for us."

On keeping down-home intimacy in a show that dazzles the senses like Floyd's laser lights orgy. Toronto Star, December 1994

"Cut back and focus on quality, focus on artists again. Everybody's got to gut-check and look in the mirror and say, "Are you here to make money until the next big fad comes along in some other city and you're going to move onto it or are you here for country music's sake?'"

On carving out a career in country music instead of being a flash in the pan. The Province, November 1995

"He told me he couldn't work with me anymore because I wasn't being myself. I had always wanted to be George Strait and that's what I was trying to do. He said the world already had a George Strait and all I could do was give them Garth Brooks."

On what his record producer, Allen Reynolds, told him when they were recording Garth's first album. The Vancouver Sun, September 1993

"Yeah, I'll stand up forever for country music. A lot of people say We Shall Be Free didn't get country radio behind it, and you got left out of the last awards show for country music.

Why do you stick up for country music?" I love country music. It's my home. I have never felt that it has slighted me. It was the format that held the ladder while I got to climb as high as I could. I don't know if you heard the story about Randy Travis. His album was selling so well that it charted on the pop charts. And his first reaction was, "Pop charts? Get it off there." I like that. I sure don't feel like a top pop performer."

On whether he feels like a representative of country music. Playboy magazine, May 1994

"Truthfully, though, this is acting. This is hard. The other stuff, the Garth stuff, it just happens, it's fun. This is work."

On his Chris Gaines CD. Vancouver Sun, July 1999

"Here's a staggering thought -- 50 per cent of the people that you knew were in radio two years ago are no longer in radio. Yeah, things have changed quite dramatically. Radio has always been the guys that have saved my butt. Now, I've got to reintroduce myself to those radio people again. The tour is the best way to do it but the tour is five months off."

On changes in radio during the years between the release of his In Pieces album and his Fresh Horses album. The Province, November 1995

"Very much so. I felt it in albums like No Fences. I felt it after the last tour as a touring artist and with the songwriting and stuff. I'm ready to move on."

On whether he feels fulfilled as an artist. Calgary Herald, January 2002

"The only regret I have . . . and I go to bed nights feeling that I am part of the blame for it . . . is somehow, somewhere we lost the guys that are the foundation of country music. We lost Haggard, we lost Jones. We lost these guys on country radio. That is the one thing that kills me. I don't know how that happened, when it happened. I just know that one day I woke up and I never heard another George Jones or Merle Haggard tune on the radio."

On no longer hearing some of the legends of country music on the radio anymore. The Province, November 1995

"When I first started, I made the mistake of wanting it to be an end-all, be-all Garth record to combine all the other records up in one. Allen saw me thinking that way and really urged me not to and just to do what we've done on the other records, just to make the record where I am at the time. And that's what we did."

On making the Scarecrow album and the influence of Allen Reynolds's advice, the producer. Calgary Herald, January 2002

"I feel very fortunate to have been in the wave of artists when labels were still developing careers. There are people who still do this. Arista Nashville president Tim DuBois with Lee Roy Parnell. He is hell bent on developing that career. And I say good for him, good for Lee Roy, good for us as country listeners because Lee Roy is a good guy. But the one-hit artists are more and more in country music when we used to never have those."

On the trend in the country music industry to focus on pumping out hits instead of crafting careers. The Province, November 1995

"I'm having a ball. Thank you all."

On winning six trophies at the Academy of Country Music Awards in 1991. The Windsor Star, April 1991

"I can't make my records for radio. I gotta make my records for the record's sake and, if radio can use it, good for all of us and, if radio can't, that's cool. I thank them for at least listening to it and making the decision."

On radio play and Fresh Horses. The Province, November 1995

"When she asked me if we could tour together, I told her I couldn't afford her. Then she did something which totally put her in a different light for me. She said, 'I'll trade the money for the chance to play in front of big crowds and promote my album.' My respect for her went through the roof."

On Trisha Yearwood not being paid for her performances on Garth's tour. The Spectator, September 1998

"It's something that I grew up on and it doesn't make like I'm selling out by doing their endorsement."

On his Scarecrow album being pushed in ads for Dr. Pepper.
Calgary Herald, January 2002

"That's how it started in Willie's in '83, playing a show for tips.
You do your big arena show, then it's funny. You come back
to that and it's come full circle."

On going from playing at Willie's Saloon in Stillwater,
Oklahoma, where he first started out to now playing at the
Wynn Las Vegas resort's Encore Theatre. The Times, October
2009

"This is actually a great opportunity that has lots of rewards
to it, and one of them is the money. Where he (Steve Wynn)
got me was his concern with the fact that my life doesn't
change. Everybody else thought money was the answer. This
guy came to me not with 'How much money is it going to take
for this to happen?' but 'What are the logistics that it's going
to take to make it happen?' That's where he started. And he
based all his decisions on either the kids or music. . . . He
figured it out real quick. He's a sharp guy."

On how Steve Wynn convinced Brooks to perform at his
resort in Las Vegas. Calgary Herald, October 2009

"Country music has huge buying power - and it's finally
getting credit for it."

On country music's surge in sales and popularity. The
Province, August 1991

"I think a lot of it has to do with '70s rock 'n' roll. I think a lot of these people that are playing the music are influenced by the '70s -- by people like the Eagles or the big bands of the '70s. And the people who are actually programming -- the radio stations, the music directors, the people at the record labels, television stations -- everyone right now is at the age where '70s rock 'n' roll was a big influence on them. I think the clearest, most evident place '70s rock 'n' roll is showing up is in '90s country."

On country music's popularity in the 1990s. Calgary Herald, May 1994

"Hopefully, we'll make the music better, get out to more people. We're trying to do stuff that nobody's heard of before, that nobody thought of before. That way, anyone who tries it after you will cite you as the one who started it. (The next album) will be totally out of left field. It'll go a lot of places I've never been to before, where I didn't think you could be. There are marriages of really different kinds of influences going on here. (The key to all this is to) take care of your music first. If you do that, the rest of the stuff will take care of itself -- all the hype, the big-mouth stuff you hear. You can't forget the heart part."

On making music in the future. The Province, December 1994

"Trisha Yearwood did me a huge favor. These guys, they had me, they had my head under water and I was dead. Trisha Yearwood gave me life with a song called In Another's Eyes."

On trying to work with his record company to get Sevens produced. Kingston Whig - Standard December 1997

"I always thought my music had to be flawless. But Reynolds taught me that sometimes you have to trade perfection for feeling."

On Nashville producer Allen Reynolds convincing him to stop trying to be a perfectionist. The Province, August 1991

"This was one of the things I didn't want to miss. The hardest part is realizing you've got 40 pounds to lose usually. I haven't eaten for about four or five days so tonight I'm going to gain about 20 pounds between midnight and four in the morning."

On performing at the Calgary Stampede in July 2012. The Canadian Press, July 2012

"The Dance. Even if I did it four times a night, I don't think I would get tired of it. It is a cool tune."

On the song he never gets tired of performing. The Vancouver Sun, April 1994

"We're probably the most flaw-filled band there is. But we like to keep the live show loose. I don't think it's fair to play the songs just the way they are on your compact disc. So we slow our ballads down and pump the fast ones up. I'm just trying to do what I'd like to hear if I were in the audience."

On his live shows, which Brooks claims are far from perfect. The Province, August 1991

"I thought I was finished."

On his career after his last album, The Chase, sold only five million copies. The Vancouver Sun, September 1993

"The cool thing about country-music fans is that they allow you to have your opinion and they can agree with it or not agree with it. It doesn't mean they're not going to buy your stuff or come out and see you play."

On the country community's reaction to him sharing controversial issues through his music. Calgary Herald, May 1994

"I want to play, I want to sing. I want the letters saying my music has rerouted somebody's life, hopefully for the better. That's what I want."

On how he prefers the music part of his career, not the business aspects. Kingston Whig - Standard, December 1997

"When this record thing went down, I didn't sleep. (I was) on the phone until 4 in the morning to London, screaming my guts out."

On the sudden closing of his record label which led to the firing of 175 EMI Records employees, some of whom were the only people Brooks trusted to launch his new album, Sevens. The Gazette, July 1997

"Oh geez. I guess the first statement right off the bat to those people is, again, don't pay the scalpers. We're gonna find a way to take care of the people who were left there in line. I'm hoping that in the years that you have seen us do what we do, that my word's good enough right now to just say please, don't buy from scalpers, we're working on a plan, and hopefully this plan will not let people down."

On hearing that that some ticket locations had 300 to 400 people still in line when tickets ran out for his concert in Dallas-Fort Worth in 1993. The Vancouver Sun, June 1993

"It's the most country album I've made but the first four singles are probably the most non-country things I've done. But we'll just get it out there and see what happens."

On his album Ropin' in the Wind. The Province, August 1991

"There's a Kiss album, Friends of Kiss, where everyone's doing their stuff and we were fortunate enough to be invited (to sing) on that album."

On collaborating with members of Kiss, who Brooks has always been a fan of. Calgary Herald, May 1994

"I can see getting the finger for this one, the state that country music is in. It's just a real two-edged sword. For some reason, rock guys can go from huge big light shows down to just two guys and a guitar and it's considered cool. Country can go from two guys and a guitar up to these big light shows and entertain people and give them their money's worth and it's considered rock 'n' roll. I don't understand where that label came from."

On the big, flashy stage show he planned to put on in Toronto in 1995. Toronto Star, December 1995

"When the term 'too country' was used for the first single, I went 'Yes!' I think all of us, especially people in the industry, never thought the four words together would be 'Garth Brooks too country.'"

On CISS-FM, Canada's largest country radio station at the time, originally refusing to play Long Neck Bottle, the first single from Sevens, claiming it was too traditional for the station's pop-oriented "new country" format. Kingston Whig - Standard, December 1997

"I know a lot of my stuff people don't consider country music; they didn't consider The Dance to be country. The Thunder Rolls was not considered country. But I can't worry about that. I know I'm country; I still love fiddle, still love (pedal) steel. We can only do what our heart tells us to do, and hopefully time will take care of whether people like it or not. Basically, I want to do something that I want to play in my truck. That's what I've made my albums on. If that isn't there, how can I expect anyone else to feel it?"

On people not always considering his music country music. The Province, December 1994

"In Sacramento we saw 62,000 people. In Vegas we saw 51,000. We just put the Fargo (North Dakota) Dome on sale, 40,000 seats, and we got two nights out of it - and they're talking about a third night because they got 385,000 calls."

On a segment of his In Pieces tour. Edmonton Journal, October 1993

"Country music is what I do. This is just something I was hired to do by the folks at Paramount. I wouldn't be doing this (otherwise)."

On his role in The Lamb as Chris Gaines. Calgary Herald, July 1999

"It's been sitting back here (pointing to the back of his head) since July 8 of '92, the day I became a father."

On how long he has been pondering retirement.   The Record, December 1995

"The week before the song came out, some select deejays did me a wonderful favor by playing the Aerosmith cover on the radio. And it got people so damned scared of it, and I was really disappointed that that happened. But Canada, for some reason, gets The Fever. Radio around here is fine with it. Maybe you guys are just listening to the song instead of that haunting word 'Aerosmith.' I appreciate it that the people are deciding it."

On his song The Fever. Toronto Star, December 1995

"This is really a nice crowd."

On the Alberta contingent during his 1996 tour. Edmonton Journal, August 1996

"It's like -- focus. And I focused, and all of a sudden the ideas for writing just started eatin' me up and I couldn't write enough. It felt like the old days."

On his longtime producer, Allen Reynolds, suggesting that it was time for Brooks to give his own music top priority again. The Spectator, November 1995

"I gotta be honest, man, I'm having the time of my life. When you stand up there on stage, and you stand next to the people you were in an old musty basement with, just dreaming, and you didn't have a pot to pee in really, and then you stand there thinking 'My God, it's happening.'"

On having fun playing music. The Gazette, January 1992

"I don't know how we do it. Maybe the fact that we're doing multiple dates and there's only one load out instead of six load outs probably saves some money. All I know is everyone's making a good living."

On making headlines for his economical ticket prices. The Spectator, September 1998

"I was shocked at how well the people received her but she came offstage dejected. I said, 'What is wrong with you?' She said, 'It just didn't work.' The next night she's doing a new number to close and the place is on its feet screaming along with her. She's going, 'Come on!' and they're screaming 'Come on!' She comes off the stage and I say, 'Wow, where'd you find that (song)?' And she said, 'Well, last night I wrote it and taught it to the band this morning and played it tonight.' That's when I knew this gal was sharper than sharp."

On Stephanie Davis, the songwriter of Wolves, opening for Brooks' tour. Edmonton Journal, October 1993

"There are big days in your career, like when you join the Grand Ole Opry... and I didn't think anything would top those. I might have lied. This may be the biggest night of my career. I'm so excited and nervous, and feel so undeserving, all at the same time."

On being inducted into the Country Music Hall of Fame and Museum in 2012. The Times, October 2012

"Playing music has never felt better or ever felt more right."

On playing a concert series at Nashville's Bridgestone Arena in December 2011 for flood relief in Tennessee. The Spectator, February 2011

"Please don't let me jinx this thing. Hopefully they can write a cheque to Feed the Children for a substantial amount around Christmastime."

On his announcement that for each new album sold between its release date and Christmas, Liberty Records will donate a dollar to Feed the Children, an Oklahoma City-based charity. The Gazette, August 1992

"For one, the price (of a used CD) is right. The consumer is right. But the money should be picked up by the retailers.

They should be paying the writers and publishers. You know, the one thing I've never understood is why people can't get it in their heads that this isn't about the artists making money. It's about the songwriters who don't. I guess people think that songwriters make millions of dollars. Songwriters are lucky to make thousands of dollars."

On his aversion to the selling of used CDs. Calgary Herald, May 1994

"Canada for me ... I know we're not the same country but I don't feel like I'm going to a different country here. I'd put anything we went through in any city in Canada up against the response we get in the United States."

On how Garth feels going to and performing in Canada. Kingston Whig - Standard December 1997

"It's great to be a part of the healing."

On his benefit concert for Nashville flood relief in 2010. Prince George Citizen, November 2010

"I don't know. I'm never there. We're always out on the road so I don't always come around."

On whether he ever feels animosity from Nashville over his vocalization against the sale of used CDs. Calgary Herald, May 1994

"You come here to work, that's the deal. We'll put you through the wringer. We want you to crawl out of here."

On what he expected of his concert go'ers in Saskatoon, Saskatchewan, in 1996. Star-Phoenix, August 1996

"We made a deal going in, and it's a deal."

On his album Sevens not being released to coincide with his August 1997 concert in New York City; without the album's release and subsequent sales, staging the massive concert will cost him more than his fee from HBO, which broadcasted the event. The Gazette, July 1997

"If you haven't seen Garth Brooks live, you're just not going to get it. I mean, all you're going to get is this guy who loves to eat and is losing his hair and wears a cowboy hat. Until you see him live, I don't think anybody understands what the GB thing is."

On the confident, aggressive performer is an alter ego that Brooks barely recognizes. The Ottawa Citizen, January 1994

"I'm hoping the tour will make a difference but if it doesn't we'll have to take a serious look at our career."

On considering retirement if a new tour doesn't stir up his fans and himself. The Vancouver Sun, March 1996

"Rock ain't what it was when I was a teen. Rock cut itself into little fragments, like dance, alternative and so on, and lost the mainstream audience. If you put too many windows in a wall, the wall falls down. I'm always arguing against those who want to cut it (country music) up into segments like new country, dance country, etc. If they keep it as one unit, the ride it's on can last 20 years."

On how he sees rock fans becoming estranged from the music and how he fears country music may go down the same path. The Province, September 1993

"It's flattering to come in second to somebody of the quality of the Beatles. But I'm sorry, the top spot belongs to country music, in my eyes. So that's what we do. We try to work toward that."

On Fresh Horses coming in second place in first week sales since The Beatles Anthology 1 was released on November 21, 1995, the same day as Fresh Horses. Toronto Star, December 1995

"One of the best shows I ever had was the early one tonight, the show right before. I went out there just to do it. The sound was perfect; it went really well. I was hoping to do it again with the second show, but brother Wynn screwed that up with his introduction!"

On doing his last two shows at Steve Wynn's resort in Las Vegas and Wynn throwing him off his game during his last show with his heartfelt introduction. The Record, November 2012

"If we're back it's because we had a good time last time."

On why he returned to play in Saskatoon, Saskatchewan. Star-Phoenix, August 1996

"It's kind of odd to be in this room. You want to be mentioned in the same breath with George Strait and Reba McEntire - those are the two heroes I grew up with. Now you're gonna get to be in the same hall with them? Make no mistake, I don't think I'm on that level. But it's pretty cool to have your name listed with them."

On being inducted into the Country Music Association's Hall of Fame. Edmonton Journal, March 2012

"These things were written to fit in our lifestyles and to go as background music. So when it came to making this album (Scarecrow), the focus isn't Garth. The focus is an American way of life."

On his songs like The Dance, which has been played at funerals and high-school graduations, or the party favourites Friends in Low Places and Two Pina Coladas. New Brunswick Telegraph Journal, November 2001

"We want people to go into the theatre and know Chris Gaines and care about Chris Gaines. The thing I'd like to get across is how serious we are about this. There's the Rutles and there's Spinal Tap and this is exactly the opposite."

On trying to establish a connection between The Lamb's future audience and Chris Gaines. Calgary Herald, July 1999

"I'm hoping we've educated some people in what country music is."

On country music. The Province, December 1994

"We'll work out deals to do two, three, four shows in each city. I'll take the family with me. We'll stay in hotels, and it'll be just like any job where you come home every night. It'll take the wind out of scalpers, too, 'cause there'll be more tickets than people."

On his 1993 world tour. The Windsor Star, December 1992

"My job is to be the most honest Garth Brooks I can be, and I say these things because I believe them. I don't think we can be free until everyone can love who they choose."

On the release of his song We Shall Be Free (with its line advocating that people "love anyone they choose"). The Vancouver Sun, September 1993

"My Mom (Capitol recording artist Colleen Carroll) gave up music for the kids. I hope I handle it as well as she did, if and when the time comes where I have to say goodbye to music because it's just taking up too much of my time that I'm not going to spend with my kids."

On upcoming potential retirement. The Record, December 1995

"What I initially wanted to do was release the album so there would be a video for each song if you played it on the DVD, but it would be adaptable so you could also listen to it on your compact disc player. When I asked Phillips how many they could manufacture, they said 12,000 a day. We're shipping six million copies. It would have taken them two-and-a-half years to fill that first order."

On his plan to make history as the first country artist to introduce digital video discs into the market with his Double Live album; technical problems put a stop to that. The Spectator, September 1998

"I feel like a part of it, but not the guy that's changing everything. Because Vince Gill is having a good year, or Clint Black, or Wynonna -- she has a lot of pop people coming over that maybe wouldn't listen to country. Then they give me a listen where they wouldn't if it weren't for Wynonna. It works both ways."

On the country explosion in the 1990s. The Province, December 1994

"It's always been about the babies. Our youngest is a junior in senior high school now. Our oldest, we just celebrated her 20th. If God lets us do it and everything goes well, I would love to tour again. I'd love to tour again with Miss Yearwood and have no guilt. But I'm still two years away."

On the possibility of touring in the future. The Canadian Press, July 2012

QUOTES ABOUT GARTH BROOKS

"He's in a category all by himself. His talent, his music, his writing, his philosophy of life, his sincerity both onstage and when you're meeting him backstage. . . . I think he's the genuine article. He's as nice as the day is long. If this man is putting on an act then give him an Academy Award because he's the best one out there."

Rod Kitter of CJWW Country 600 in Saskatoon, Saskatchewan, on Garth. Star-Phoenix, August 1996

"This thing is literally either going to make him or break him. I can tell you, having been pretty much in the position he's in, that you get there and you realize that you're not doing anything new. You know you can only go downhill from there. So you step out and you take chances."

Kenny Rogers on Garth's Chris Gaines phase. Niagara Falls Review, September 1999

"If Garth Brooks thinks being with his wife when she's having a baby is more important than a piece of plastic and metal, I don't know where his values are."

Jay Leno (jokingly) on Brooks being absent from the 1994 CMA awards as his wife was giving birth to August Anna the same night. Kitchener - Waterloo Record, May 1994

"I don't understand why he didn't just make the kind of new music he wanted to make as Garth Brooks. But I've known Garth for a long time and I can tell you this. When he decides to do something, he's determined."

Vince Gill on Garth's Chris Gaines phase. The Spectator, September 1999

"Garth is both incapable and unwilling to transform himself slightly into a pop star as Shania (Twain) did. What he has done is cut himself down the middle, trying to preserve like jelly the old Garth, which has changed almost none in 10 years. He's creating the pop persona because what Garth wants ultimately is not money or fame or groupies. It's power. He wants to be this icon. He's got two-thirds of the country with him, but there is this other third. Garth thinks he is protecting the franchise of Garth Brooks by making Chris Gaines. In fact, he's making Garth much more vulnerable by opening up the recesses."

Bruce Feiler, a writer who parlayed his Esquire profile of Brooks into a critically acclaimed book, Dreaming Out Loud. The Spectator, September 1999

"Garth has a lot of fans in the Padres family. He earned our respect by the way he handled himself in Peoria last year. Right now he's driven. He's working very hard. People in the music business told me he was like that."

Kevin Towers, general manager of the San Diego Padres, on Garth. New Brunswick Telegraph Journal, March 1999

"It's expensive to take a record to the top. So why spend that money to have a pop hit when Garth's already selling more records than Guns N' Roses? We've never had an act like Garth as long as I've been in Nashville. Garth doesn't need to cross over. He has crossed over, just because he's so huge."

Tony Brown, a senior vice-president at MCA's Nashville division, on Garth and claims that they are trying to get him to cross over to the pop realm. The Gazette, January 1992

"We look for people who are really energetic. It's instant gratification when you see people cry and get so excited."

Elaina Gustat, one of Garth's crew members, who combs the bleachers before a concert starts looking for the chosen few diehard fans to invite on Garth's behalf to sit in row one instead of remain in the nosebleed area. Edmonton Journal, August 1996

"It's Garth madness! It's been a really exciting day. There's such energy around Brooks."

Heather MacDonald, marketing director for Vancouver-based Perryscope Concert Productions, when Garth's two Edmonton, Alberta, concerts sold out in one hour, prompting the addition of a third show. Edmonton Journal, June 1996

"It's a good thing that he can sing because he sure doesn't look good in a uniform. And he runs like he's spent too much time on the back of a horse."

Frank Viola, former New York Mets pitcher, on Garth's baseball abilities. Calgary Herald, March 2000

"I love his stuff, don't get me wrong. I would rather play with him than a lot of country artists ... but I've also done Janis Joplin, Bonnie Raitt, Aretha Franklin, you know, I'm kind of like a Woodstock baby."

Betsy Brooks, Garth's big sister, who toured with her brother's band from 1990 to 1995 when she left the band to promote her own debut album. The Spectator, March 1995

"One gifted son of a gun."

Steve Wynn on Garth. The Record, November 2012

"Someone who has been as driven as he is is likely to reappear in some way or other. I don't think someone like Garth is going to be comfortable being retired for very long."

Ed Benson, executive director of the Country Music Association, on Garth's retirement in 1999. The Province, December 1999

"I think (the price of) CDs are too high. So are concert tickets. That's why I'm impressed with Garth Brooks. He keeps his ticket prices down because he cares about his fans. I like his style."

Charlie Daniels, a fiddler best known for his hit The Devil Went Down to Georgia, on what impresses him most about Garth. Calgary Herald, August 1997

"He's driven. The guy has more charisma than should be legally allowed. There's nothing he isn't involved with, nothing I know of. Garth kinda threw away the rule book on the normal protocol on how you have a career."

John McBride, country star Martina McBride's husband and Garth's tour production manager, on Garth. The Province, July 1996

"There's two risky elements here. Can Garth succeed in the rock, pop, and R&B world? And can you put out an advance soundtrack and succeed without the benefit of the movie being in theatres? And that doesn't even address the challenge of him acting."

Pat Quigley, president of Capitol Nashville, on Garth's portrayal of Chris Gaines and his role in the movie The Lamb. Calgary Herald, July 1999

"Garth's fans will love him for it . . . and everyone else will be left wondering why anyone cares."

David Howell, music writer, on Brooks' album, In Pieces. Edmonton Journal, October 1993

"Garth is a very unique person and he does things for who knows what reasons. I still don't really know what propelled him to do that. I think he loves to help people and saw something in me that made him feel that I deserved this opportunity. I don't know if I do deserve it but I'm real thankful that he apparently thought I did."

Martina McBride on Garth taking her from a booth selling t-shirts on his tour to making her his opening singing act. The Times, August 1993

"I don't know if there's anybody who's received more honours and I've never seen anyone so excited. I've never seen him as excited about such an honour."

Trisha Yearwood on Garth's induction into the Country Music Hall of Fame & Museum in Nashville. Alberni Valley Times, October 2012

"He's taking a hiatus. Please don't use the word retiring, he's definitely not. He's very blunt about that. He's taking a break. Everybody needs time to do that."

Karen Byrd, publicist for Garth Brooks, on mentioning the word 'retirement' in the same sentence as 'Garth Brooks'. The Province, October 1998

"A lot of people think country music started with Garth Brooks, which is great - Garth recruited a lot of people. But it means a whole lot to me, while I have their attention, to tell them the truth."

Marty Stuart on country music's rich history which predates Garth Brooks. Edmonton Journal, March 1993

"He has one of the nicest crews I've ever seen. There's not been a cross word spoken. He has a knack for hiring great people. The way they work together, it's something to see."

Stephanie Davis, Garth's opening act on his 1993 tour, on life with the Brooks crew. Calgary Herald, October 1993

"I don't think anybody knows what will happen. But the thing that you have to admire about Garth is that he's working very hard. If he makes a mistake, he's learning from it."

Tony Gwynn, a San Diego Padres ballplayer, on Garth. New Brunswick Telegraph Journal, March 1999

"It's meant so much to me that Garth has mentioned me over the years as one of his influences."

James Taylor on Garth often speaking of him and naming his daughter, Taylor, after the artist.   The Times, October 2012

"I've seen him a few times before, but this time it was really special. It was just us teammates and Garth got so into it. He told so many funny stories about how he grew up. He's just got such a great way about him and he's a really down-to-earth guy. It's like talking to one of your buddies back home . . . . And he sounds so good live."

Adrian Aucoin, Calgary Flames defenseman, on a private concert Garth put on in a Calgary restaurant to thank the team for their generous donation to his Teammates For Kids Foundation. Calgary Herald, March 2009

"We got together the following Saturday after meeting and we spent the whole day playing and I thought his name was Garf. I had never heard of a Garth before. So, for two weeks I was calling him Garf and he's so polite he never corrected me."

Ty England, Garth's guitarist for seven years, on his first few meetings with Garth after meeting him at a cafe during their days together at Oklahoma State. Calgary Herald, July 1995

"Clearly this guy got run over by the crazy truck and I'm talking all 18 wheels."

Critic Robert Sheffield writing in Rolling Stone on Brooks taking on the persona of a fictitious Australian rock star, Chris Gaines. The Record, September 1999

Hope you've enjoyed this round-up of Garth's thoughts on his life, his loves, and music.

Have a great day!

Dream big,
Toby

Printed in Great Britain
by Amazon.co.uk, Ltd.,
Marston Gate.